I WANT YOU TO KNOW ME...

Blessings!
Vickie Mullins

I WANT YOU TO KNOW ME...

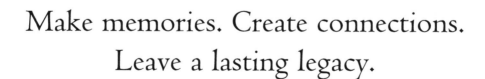

Love, Mom & Dad

Make memories. Create connections.
Leave a lasting legacy.

Vickie Mullins

AZURE EYES PUBLISHING

Scottsdale, Arizona

www.IWantYouToKnowMe.com

10 9 8 7 6 5 4 3 2 1

Copyright © 2006 Vickie Mullins

Published by
Azure Eyes Publishing
4848 E. Cactus, Ste. 505-118
Scottsdale, AZ 85254-4163

480-941-8202

www.IWantYouToKnowMe.com

Book Design: Mullins Creative, Inc., Brandi Hollister

Quotes copyright, "Worth Repeating: More than 5,000 Classic and Contemporary Quotes" by Bob Kelly

This book is a non-fiction work. Any personal reference to actual people is with permission.

ISBN 0-9769923-4-5

This book
is dedicated to my husband

Jack

who, when completing the Dad section of this book,
responded to "What is your favorite smell?"
with this answer
"Any fragrance on my love's neck."
Every woman should be so blessed!

and to the memory of

Shelly Reklaitis

the angel inspiration of this book

Other books in this series for every loved one in your family ...

Grandma &
Grandpa

Mom

Dad

Grandpa

Grandma

Me

Your
American Hero

Order at www.IWantYouToKnowMe.com

Acknowledgements

I Want You To Know Me ... was not planned by anyone on this earth, but I believe God, in His infinite wisdom planned it long ago. As I look back over my life, I can see where He led me to get the experience and learn the lessons I would need to be able to complete this project. It is not my idea, it is His. He placed the passion so deep in my heart, that I had no choice but to do it. Then He surrounded me with everyone I needed to accomplish the task at hand.

The greatest thanks go to my husband Jack; he has always been there for me, loving me and patiently listening as I shared another idea with him. Jack's the one who has always given me the support and confidence to tackle anything.

To my children – Jonathan and Shannon – you are just like Dad, you are just like me, you make everything worthwhile.

To Mom, Dad, Dianne and Patrick, thank you from the bottom of my heart for your unconditional love. You have been the safety net that has always been there to catch me.

I express my gracious thanks to my La Casa de Cristo friends. Especially to Jim & Susan McGiffert and Jennine Ulibarri who believed in me and kept the encouragement coming through the hardest times. I will be forever grateful.

I would like to acknowledge Michelle Cubas who served as the mid-wife bringing this project to life. And to Raleigh Pinskey who jumped on board to lead the charge of sharing these books with the world, you're the best.

A special thank you to Brandi Hollister and Tom Howard for contributing their incredible design talents to turn the idea into a visual reality.

And thank you to Paul Reklaitis for allowing me in to his family's life as it turned upside down. Your trust and openness enabled Shelly's legacy to live on.

Foreword

The fabric of a family is not so much woven with memories, it's woven together with innies and outies, bushy eyebrows, and laughs that sound alike for generations. These are the threads that define us as individuals yet join us as families. They link our hearts and link our souls from generation to generation. Readers have described this book as the ultimate family show and tell book. So find yourself a comfortable chair and get ready to discover the oo's, the ah's and the aha's that create a lasting legacy.

Readers tell us they use it to initiate a family dialogue.

Even the closest families most likely haven't shared the answers to many of the questions contained within these covers. Gather your loved ones around a table and let the conversations begin. The extra lines below each question will allow for multiple entries.

For some, the experience of creating a personal legacy keeps their memories alive.

Life is unpredictable, none of us knows for sure what the future holds. By taking the time now to record this information, those who are left behind after a loved one's death will have everything they need to know to make a connection that will last forever. It is a precious gift of oneself that cannot be replaced.

For others, it is a vehicle to reach out to family members.

Families will find this book a valuable resource and opportunity to rekindle and rebuild relationships that have faded.

I encourage you to be generous with the information you provide; the more you share, the stronger your connection can, and will be.

I WANT YOU TO KNOW ME...

Love, Mom

For Dad's connection,
turn to page 77.

This book is about
making a connection to:

_____

(Mom, write your name here)

Mom,

place a photograph

of you here.

Section One

❤ physical characteristics

❤ What color is your hair?

....

....

....

....

....

....

❤ Is your hair thick or thin?

....

....

....

....

....

....

....

The average person
has 100,000 hairs
on his/her head.

❤ Do you have a widow's peak?

....

....

....

....

....

....

....

❤ Where does your hair part naturally, on the left, center or right?

....

....

....

....

....

....

❤ Is your hair curly or straight?

....

....

....

....

....

....

My mom always told me, "Eat the crusts on your bread or your curls will go away."
Take a look at the back cover —
I must've eaten my crusts!
– Vickie Mullins

❤ Do you have any cowlicks?

....

....

....

....

....

....

....

❤ Are your earlobes attached at the base?

....

....

....

....

....

....

....

❤ Do your ears stick out or do they lay flat?

....

....

....

....

....

....

....

*The one who listens
is the one who
understands.*
~ African Proverb

❤ Are your ears pierced?

....

....

....

....

....

....

If your ears are
pierced, how
many piercings
do you have in
each ear?

....

....

....

❤ Is your face round, oval or square?

....

....

....

....

....

....

....

Family faces are
magic mirrors.
Looking at people
who belong to us,
we see the past,
present and future.
We make discoveries
about ourselves.

~ Gail Lument Buckley

❤ Do you have high cheek bones?

....

....

....

....

....

....

....

❤ Do you have a large or small forehead?

....

....

....

....

....

....

....

❤ Do you have dimples?

....

....

If you do have
dimples, where
are they?

....

....

....

....

....

....

....

....

❤ Do you have any freckles?

....

....

....

....

....

....

....

Some people believe freckles are left from kisses by angels.

❤ What color are your eyes?

....

....

....

....

....

....

....

❤ What shape are your eyes?

....

....

....

....

....

....

....

Our eyes remain the same size from birth.

❤ Do you wear contacts, eyeglasses or neither?

....

....

....

....

....

If you wear contacts or glasses, are you far-sighted or near-sighted?

....

....

....

Your nose and ears
never stop growing.

❤ Is your nose big or small?

....

....

....

....

....

....

....

❤ Is your nose pointy or rounded?

....

....

....

....

....

....

....

💗 Are your lips thin or full?

....

....

....

....

....

....

....

Leonardo da Vinci took 10 years to paint Mona Lisa's lips.

💗 Are your teeth naturally crooked or straight?

....

....

....

....

....

....

Did you ever wear braces on your teeth?

....

....

....

For how long?

....

Famous females
with a cleft in their
chins include
Ashlee Simpson
and Jamie Pressley.

❤ Do you have a cleft in your chin?

....

....

....

....

....

....

❤ Is your chin pointed or round?

....

....

....

....

....

....

....

❤ Do you have a unibrow?

....

....

....

....

....

....

....

❤ Do you have long or short eyelashes?

....

....

....

....

....

....

....

❤ Do you squint when you smile?

....

....

....

....

....

....

A smile is the shortest distance between two people.
~ Victor Borge

❤ Do you show your gums when you smile?

....

....

....

....

....

....

❤ Are you big-boned or petite?

....

....

....

....

....

....

....

❤ Do you have thick or thin ankles?

....

....

....

....

....

....

❤ Do you have thick or thin wrists?

....

....

....

....

....

....

....

❤ How tall are you?

....

....

....

....

....

....

....

Women in the smallest pygmy tribe in Zaire average 4'5" tall.

❤ Do you have an "inny" or "outy" belly button?

....

....

....

....

....

....

❤ Do you have a long or short trunk?

....

....

....

....

....

....

❤ Do you have long legs or short legs?

....

....

....

....

....

....

❤ Do you have lots of hair on your body or just a little?

Men lose about 40 hairs a day. Women lose about 70 hairs a day.

....

....

....

....

....

❤ Do you use a razor. If you use a razor, is it electric?

....

....

....

....

....

....

❤ Are you high-waisted or low-waisted?

....

....

....

....

....

....

❤ Are your arms long, short or medium?

....

....

....

....

....

....

....

❤ Do you cross your arms right-over-left or left-over-right?

....

....

....

....

....

....

❤ What is your ring size?

....

....

....

....

....

....

....

❤ Are you allergic to anything?

....

....

....

....

....

....

The following eight foods account for 90% of all food-allergic reactions: milk, egg, peanut and tree nuts (walnut, cashew, etc.), fish, shellfish, soy and wheat.

❤ Are you coordinated or clumsy?

....

....

....

....

....

....

....

❤ Is your skin smooth or rough?

....

....

....

....

....

....

💜 Are your fingers and toes long or short?

....

....

....

....

....

....

....

💜 Do you have straight or curved thumbs?

....

....

....

....

....

....

An old wive's tale suggests that if a woman has a curved thumb, she will rule the household. Oh, really????

❤ Are your fingernails strong or weak?

....

....

....

....

....

....

....

Fingernails grow nearly 4 times faster than toenails.

❤ Do you bite your fingernails?

....

....

....

....

....

....

....

❤ Are you right handed or left handed?

....

....

....

....

....

....

....

❤ Are your second toes longer than your big toes?

....

....

....

....

....

....

❤ What is your shoe size?

....

....

....

....

....

....

....

❤ Are your feet wide or narrow?

....

....

....

....

....

....

....

❤ Do you have a deep voice or a high voice?

....

....

....

....

....

....

❤ Can you sing well?

....

....

....

....

....

....

A friend hears the song of the heart and sings it when memory fails.

~ Martin Luther

Make memories. Create connections. Leave a lasting legacy.   **29**

❤ Can you whistle with just your lips?

....

....

....

....

....

....

....

❤ Can you whistle using your fingers?

....

....

....

....

....

....

❤ Can you roll your Rs?

....

....

....

....

....

....

....

❤ Can you touch your tongue to your nose?

....

....

....

....

....

Your tongue is the strongest muscle in your body.

❤ Can you roll your tongue?

....

....

....

....

....

....

Or are you even
more special
and have the
ability to turn it
into a "w"?

....

❤ Can you wiggle your ears?

....

....

....

....

....

....

....

❤ Can you wiggle your nose?

....

....

....

....

....

....

....

❤ Can you flare your nostrils?

....

....

....

....

....

....

....

❤ Can you blow a bubble with gum?

....

....

....

....

....

....

....

According to Guinness World Records, the greatest diameter for a bubble gum bubble is 23".

❤ Do you have a unique physical characteristic?

....

....

....

....

....

....

❤ Are you limber or stiff?

....

....

....

....

....

....

....

❤ Have you ever been able to do a
cartwheel?

....

....

....

....

....

....

❤ Have you ever been able to do a hand stand?

What about
a head stand?

....

....

....

....

....

....

....

....

....

❤ Can you bend over and touch your toes?

....

....

....

....

....

....

....

❤ Do you sunburn or go directly to tan?

....

....

....

....

....

....

....

❤ Is your skin fair, more olive or dark?

....

....

....

....

....

....

....

❤ What is your blood type?

O positive is the
most common blood
type, AB negative
is the rarest.

....

....

....

....

....

....

....

Section Two

♥ **personal details and preferences**

♥ Are you energetic or calm?

....

....

....

....

....

....

❤ Are you a morning person or a night owl?

I have never known an early riser to be compelled to hurry.

~ J.B. Chapman

....

....

....

....

....

....

❤ Are you a deep sleeper or a light sleeper?

....

....

....

....

....

....

❤ What do you wear to sleep in?

....

....

....

....

....

....

....

❤ What is your favorite sleeping position?

....

....

....

....

....

....

....

Only humans sleep
on their backs.

Are your pillows
soft or hard?

....

....

....

❤ Do you sleep with one pillow or
multiple pillows?

....

....

....

....

....

....

❤ Do you like a soft or hard mattress?

....

....

....

....

....

....

....

❤ Do you fall asleep when your head hits the pillow or does it take awhile to doze off?

....

....

....

....

....

....

The average person falls asleep in seven minutes.

❤ Do you like to sleep in a cold room with lots of covers or a warm room with few covers?

....

....

....

....

....

....

Did you know that on average, a person spends about 122 days a year sleeping?

❤ How many hours of sleep per night do you need to feel rested?

....

....

....

....

....

....

❤ Are you a leader or a follower?

....

....

....

....

....

....

❤ Do you prefer silence, music or TV as background around the house?

....

....

....

....

....

....

❤ Are you usually late or early?

....

....

....

....

....

....

❤ Where are you ticklish?

....
....
....
....
....
....

Scientists have found that it is impossible to tickle yourself. A region in the posterior portion of the brain warns the rest of your brain when you are attempting to tickle yourself.

❤ Are you an aggressive or defensive driver?

....
....
....
....
....
....

❤ Do you have a nervous habit?

....

....

....

....

....

....

....

❤ Do you have a habit you'd like to break?

....

....

....

....

....

....

❤ What makes you laugh?

....

....

....

....

....

....

....

The most completely lost of all days is the one on which we have not laughed.

~ Anonymous

❤ Are you a good speller?

....

....

....

....

....

....

....

❤ Do you prefer baths or showers?

....

....

....

....

....

....

....

Water consumption averages 7-10 gallons for showers, baths average 20 gallons.

❤ Do you bathe in the morning or in the evening?

....

....

....

....

....

❤ What makes you cry?

Tears are the safety valve of the heart when too much pressure is laid on.

~ Albert Smith

....

....

....

....

....

....

....

❤ Are you messy or neat?

....

....

....

....

....

....

....

❤ What are you afraid of?

....

....

....

....

....

....

....

❤ What leg do you put into your pants first?

....

....

....

....

....

....

❤ What type of music do you prefer?

....

....

....

....

....

....

My heart, which is
full to overflowing,
has often been
solaced and
refreshed by
music when sick
and weary.
~ Martin Luther

❤ Do you prefer the mountains or
the beach?

....

....

....

....

....

....

❤ What is your favorite color?

....

....

....

....

....

....

....

According to Crayola®, America's favorite crayon color is blue.

❤ What is your favorite holiday?

....

....

....

....

....

....

....

❤ What is your favorite weather?

....

....

....

....

....

....

❤ Do you have a favorite pet?

No symphony orchestra ever played music like a two-year-old girl laughing with a puppy.

~ Bern Williams

....

....

....

....

....

....

❤ What is your favorite wild animal?

....

....

....

....

....

....

....

❤ What is your favorite smell?

....

....

....

....

....

....

....

How about bread baking or line-dried cotton sheets or baby's breath or the smell after a rain or ...

❤ Are you an outdoor or an indoor person?

....

....

....

....

....

....

....

❤ What is your favorite season?

....

....

....

....

....

....

❤ Would you rather vacation in a tent or a hotel?

....

....

....

....

....

....

❤ What is your favorite flower?

....

....

....

....

....

....

God gave us our memories so we might have roses in December.

~ James. M. Barrie

❤ Do you prefer to dress up or dress down?

....

....

....

....

....

....

....

❤ Do you like surprises?

....

....

....

....

....

....

....

♥ In your family, are you the oldest, youngest, middle, in-between, or only child?

....

....

....

....

....

....

If you're in-between, where are you in the order?

....

....

....

♥ Do you like being alone or with a group?

....

....

....

....

....

....

....

❤ Is your glass half empty or half full?

....

....

....

....

....

....

....

❤ Are you organized or disorganized?

....

....

....

....

....

....

....

❤ Are you a list maker?

....

....

....

....

....

....

....

❤ Are you patient or impatient?

....

....

....

....

....

....

....

❤ Are you a doer or a procrastinator?

....

....

....

....

....

....

....

❤ Are you shy or outgoing?

....

....

....

....

....

....

....

❤ What kinds of snacks do you like?

....

....

....

....

....

....

....

❤ What is your favorite hot beverage?

....

....

....

....

....

....

....

Make memories. Create connections. Leave a lasting legacy.   **63**

❤ What is your favorite cold beverage?

....

....

....

....

....

....

....

❤ Is your favorite meal breakfast, lunch or dinner?

The first thing
I remember liking
that liked me back
was food.

~ Rhoda Morgenstern

....

....

....

....

....

....

❤ What do you like on your hamburgers?

....

....

....

....

....

....

....

❤ What is your favorite fruit?

....

....

....

....

....

....

....

❤ What is your favorite vegetable?

....

....

....

....

....

....

❤ What is your favorite food ... and your least favorite?

Enough is as good as a feast.

– Maddy Ross

....

....

....

....

....

❤ Do you like food hot & spicy or mild?

....

....

....

....

....

....

....

❤ What do you like on your pizza?

....

....

....

....

....

....

....

Americans, on the average, eat 18 acres of pizza every day.

❤ What is your favorite ice cream topping?

....

....

....

....

....

....

....

❤ What is your favorite sport to watch?

....

....

....

....

....

....

....

Sports do not build character. They reveal it.

~ Heywood Broun

❤ Can you juggle?

....

....

....

....

....

....

....

❤ What is your favorite sport to play?

....

....

....

....

....

....

....

❤ Do you like to read?

If you like to
read, what types
of books do
you prefer?

....

....

....

....

....

....

....

....

....

....

❤ Are you creative or analytical?

....

....

....

....

....

....

....

❤ Can you swim?

....

....

....

....

....

....

....

❤ Have you ever done a flip off a
diving board?

....

....

....

....

....

....

❤ Have you ever been able to do the splits?

....

....

....

....

....

....

....

❤ Can you play a musical instrument?

If so, did you ever take lessons on this instrument?

....

....

....

And for how long?

....

....

....

....

....

....

❤ What was your favorite subject in school?

....

....

....

....

....

....

....

School is a building that has four walls—with tomorrow inside.

~ Lon Watters

❤ Can you keep a secret?

....

....

....

....

....

....

....

❤ Do you remember other people's names or faces best?

....

....

....

....

....

....

❤ Do you talk to yourself out loud?

....

....

....

....

....

....

....

❤ Use this space for anything else you may want to share.

....

....

....

....

....

....

....

....

....

....

....

....

....

Good, better, best,
never let it rest,
until your good is
better, and
your better, best.
~ Aunt Dorothy

A 14 year-old's revelation brings Dad closer

Veronica was an only child with two parents who loved her dearly. As she had grown up, a special bond had developed between her and her Mom as they shared their "girly" activities. Dad had always been there for her, but as the only guy in the house, he'd always been sort of on the outside looking in.

When Veronica's Mom announced that she and Dad would be filling out *I Want You To Know Me* that Sunday afternoon, Veronica offered her assistance. During the next couple of hours, the mother and daughter laughed together as Mom shared her answers to the curious questions.

As they finished up, Veronica took the book and headed off to find her Dad, it was his turn to complete the pages with her.

Afternoon had turned into early evening when Veronica and her Dad emerged from the study, both grinning from ear to ear. "Guess what I found out Mom. I'm not just like you, I'm just like my Dad!" exclaimed Veronica.

Veronica's Mom shared this story with me a couple weeks after they'd completed the book. She went on to say that their family would never be the same. The time they had spent answering the simple questions had not only gifted Veronica by opening her eyes to who she really was, but, her Dad was blessed as well when a new connection was made between father and daughter. They now share a new closeness and Dad no longer feels he is the odd man out.

I WANT YOU TO KNOW ME...

Love, Dad

For Mom's connection,
turn to page 1.

This book is about making a connection to:

_____

(Dad, write your name here)

Dad,

place a photograph

of you here.

Section One

♥ physical characteristics

♥ *What color is your hair?*

....

....

....

....

....

....

❤ Is your hair thick or thin?

....

....

....

....

....

....

....

❤ Is your hair curly or straight?

....

....

....

....

....

....

....

❤ Where does your hair part naturally, on the left, center or right?

....

....

....

....

....

....

❤ Are you balding?

....

....

....

....

....

....

The average person has 100,000 hairs on his/her head.

❤ Do you have any cowlicks?

....

....

....

....

....

....

....

❤ Are your earlobes attached at the base?

....

....

....

....

....

....

....

❤ Do your ears stick out or do they lay flat?

....

....

....

....

....

....

....

Listen, or thy tongue will keep thee deaf.
~ Native American Proverb

❤ Are your ears pierced?

....

....

....

....

....

....

....

Family faces are
magic mirrors.
Looking at people
who belong to us,
we see the past,
present and future.
We make discoveries
about ourselves.

~ Gail Lumen Buckle

❤ Is your face round, oval or square?

....

....

....

....

....

....

❤ Do you have a prominent Adam's apple?

....

....

....

....

....

....

❤ Do you have a large or small forehead?

....

....

....

....

....

....

❤ Do you have dimples?

....

....

....

....

....

....

If you do have dimples, where are they?

....

....

....

❤ Do you have any freckles?

Some people believe freckles are left from kisses by angels.

....

....

....

....

....

....

....

❤ What color are your eyes?

....

....

....

....

....

....

....

❤ What shape are your eyes?

....

....

Our eyes remain the
same size from birth.

....

....

....

....

....

❤ Do you wear contacts, eyeglasses
or neither?

*If you wear
contacts or
glasses, are you
far-sighted or
near-sighted?*

....

....

....

....

....

....

....

....

❤ Is your nose pointed or round?

....

....

....

....

....

....

....

❤ Is your nose big or small?

....

....

....

....

....

....

❤ Are your lips thin or full?

....

....

....

....

....

....

....

Leonardo da Vinci took 10 years to paint Mona Lisa's lips.

❤ Are your teeth naturally crooked or straight?

....

....

....

....

....

Did you ever wear braces on your teeth?

....

....

....

For how long?

....

❤ Do you have a cleft in your chin?

Famous men
with a cleft in
their chins include
Kirk Douglas,
Abraham Lincoln,
Cary Grant &
John Travolta.

....

....

....

....

....

....

❤ Is your chin pointed or round?

....

....

....

....

....

....

❤ Do you have a unibrow?

....

....

....

....

....

....

....

❤ Do you have long or short eyelashes?

....

....

....

....

....

....

....

❤ Do you squint when you smile?

....

....

....

....

....

....

If you can't do anything else to help along, just smile.

~ Eleanor Kirk

❤ Do you have a heavy or light beard?

....

....

....

....

....

....

❤ Have you ever grown a moustache, beard or goatee?

....

....

....

....

....

....

❤ Do you have thick or thin wrists ... what about thick or thin ankles?

....

....

....

....

....

❤ How tall are you?

....
....
....
....
....
....

The average height for American men today is 5'7".

❤ Do you have long legs or short legs?

....
....
....
....
....
....

❤ Do you have lots of hair on your body or just a little?

....

....

....

....

....

....

Men lose about 40 hairs a day. Women lose about 70 hairs a day.

❤ Do you use a razor?

....

....

....

....

....

....

If you use a razor, is it electric?

....

....

....

❤ Are you high-waisted or low-waisted?

....

....

....

....

....

....

❤ Do you have an "inny" or "outy" belly button?

....

....

....

....

....

....

❤ Do you have a long or short trunk?

....

....

....

....

....

....

....

❤ Are your arms long, short or medium?

....

....

....

....

....

....

❤ Do you cross your arms right-over-left or left-over-right?

....

....

....

....

....

....

❤ What is your ring size?

....

....

....

....

....

....

....

❤ Are you allergic to anything?

....

....

....

....

....

....

....

The following eight foods account for 90% of all food-allergic reactions: milk, egg, peanut and tree nuts (walnut, cashew, etc.), fish, shellfish, soy and wheat.

❤ Are you coordinated or clumsy?

....

....

....

....

....

....

....

❤ Is your skin smooth or rough?

....

....

....

....

....

....

....

❤ Are your fingers and toes long or short?

....

....

....

....

....

....

....

❤ Do you have straight or curved thumbs?

....

....

....

....

....

....

....

❤ Are your fingernails strong or weak?

....

....

....

....

....

....

**Fingernails grow
nearly 4 times faster
than toenails.**

❤ Do you bite your fingernails?

....

....

....

....

....

....

....

❤ Are you right handed or left handed?

....

....

....

....

....

....

International
left-handers day
is August 13.

❤ Are your second toes longer than your big toes?

....

....

....

....

....

....

❤ What is your shoe size?

....

....

....

....

....

....

❤ Are your feet wide or narrow?

....

....

....

....

....

....

....

❤ Do you have a deep voice or a high voice?

Do you sing
bass, tenor
or baritone?

....

....

....

....

....

....

....

....

....

❤ Can you sing well?

....

....

....

....

....

....

....

❤ Can you whistle with just your lips?

....

....

....

....

....

....

❤ Can you whistle using your fingers?

....

....

....

....

....

....

....

❤ Can you roll your Rs?

....

....

....

....

....

....

❤ Can you touch your tongue to your nose?

....

....

....

....

....

....

....

Your tongue is the strongest muscle in your body.

❤ Can you roll your tongue?

....

....

....

....

....

Or are you even more special and have the ability to turn it into a "w"?

....

....

....

❤ Can you wiggle your ears?

....

....

....

....

....

....

....

❤ Can you wiggle your nose?

....

....

....

....

....

....

....

❤ Can you flare your nostrils?

....

....

....

....

....

....

....

❤ Can you blow a bubble with gum?

....

....

....

....

....

....

According to Guinness World Records, the greatest diameter for a bubble gum bubble is 23".

❤ Do you have a unique physical characteristic?

....

....

....

....

....

....

❤ Are you limber or stiff?

....

....

....

....

....

....

❤ Have you ever been able to do
a cartwheel?

....

....

....

....

....

....

❤ Have you ever been able to do a
hand stand?

What about
a head stand?

....

....

....

....

....

....

❤ Can you bend over and touch your toes?

....

....

....

....

....

....

....

❤ Is your skin fair, more olive or dark?

....

....

....

....

....

....

❤ *Do you sunburn or go directly to tan?*

....

....

....

....

....

....

❤ What is your blood type?

....

....

....

....

....

....

O positive is the most common blood type, AB negative is the rarest.

Section Two

♥ physical characteristics

♥ Are you energetic or calm?

....

....

....

....

....

....

❤ Are you a morning person or a night owl?

I have never known an early riser to be compelled to hurry.

~ J.B. Chapman

....

....

....

....

....

....

❤ Are you a deep sleeper or a light sleeper?

How many hours of sleep do you need to feel rested?

....

....

....

....

....

....

....

....

❤ What do you wear to sleep?

....

....

....

....

....

....

....

❤ What is your favorite sleeping position?

....

....

....

....

....

....

Only humans sleep
on their backs.

❤ Do you sleep with one pillow or multiple pillows?

Are your pillows soft or hard?

....

....

....

....

....

....

....

....

....

❤ Do you like a soft or hard mattress?

Did you know that on average, a person spends about 122 days a year sleeping?

....

....

....

....

....

....

....

❤ Do you fall asleep when your head hits the pillow or does it take awhile to doze off?

....

....

....

....

....

....

The average person falls asleep in seven minutes.

❤ Do you like to sleep in a cold room with lots of covers or a warm room with few covers?

....

....

....

....

....

....

Scientists have found that it is impossible to tickle yourself. A region in the posterior portion of the brain, warns the rest of your brain when you are attempting to tickle yourself.

❤ Where are you ticklish?

....

....

....

....

....

....

....

❤ Are you a leader or a follower?

....

....

....

....

....

....

....

❤ Do you have a nervous habit?

....

....

....

....

....

....

❤ Do you have a habit you'd like to break?

....

....

....

....

....

....

❤ What makes you laugh?

....

....

....

....

....

....

....

Nothing is more significant of men's character than what they laugh at.

~ Johann von Goethe

❤ Are you a good speller?

....

....

....

....

....

....

....

❤ Do you prefer to shower in the morning or evening?

....

....

....

....

....

....

Water consumption averages 7-10 gallons for showers, baths average 20 gallons.

❤ What makes you cry?

....

....

....

....

....

....

Tears are often the telescope through which men see far into heaven.

~ Henry Ward Beecher

❤ Are you messy or neat?

....

....

....

....

....

....

....

❤ What are you afraid of?

....

....

....

....

....

....

....

Never fear shadows. They simply mean there's a light shining somewhere.

~ Ruth E. Renkel

❤ Are you an aggressive or defensive driver?

....

....

....

....

....

....

....

❤ Are you usually late or early?

....

....

....

....

....

....

❤ What leg do you put into your pants first?

....

....

....

....

....

....

❤ What type of music do you prefer?

....

....

....

....

....

....

❤ Can you play a musical instrument?

....

....

....

....

....

....

....

If so, did you ever take lessons on this instrument?

....

....

....

❤ Do you prefer silence, music or TV as background around the house?

....

....

....

....

....

....

Make memories. Create connections. Leave a lasting legacy.

There are no words
in the dictionary
that rhyme with
purple, orange
or silver.

❤ What is your favorite color?

....

....

....

....

....

....

❤ What is your favorite holiday?

....

....

....

....

....

....

❤ What is your favorite weather?

....

....

....

....

....

....

....

❤ What is your favorite domestic animal?

....

....

....

....

....

....

❤ What is your favorite wild animal?

....

....

....

....

....

....

....

❤ What is your favorite smell?

....

....

*How about
bread baking or
freshly cut grass
or meat cookin'
on the grill ...*

....

....

....

....

❤ Are you an outdoor or an indoor person?

....

....

....

....

....

....

....

❤ What is your favorite season?

....

....

....

....

....

....

My dad's favorite season was always "huntin' season."

❤ Would you rather vacation in a tent or a hotel?

....

....

....

....

....

He can climb the highest mountain or swim the biggest ocean. He can fly the fastest plane and fight the strongest tiger. My father can do anything! But most of the time he just carries out the garbage.

~ Anonymous
8-year-old

❤ Do you prefer the mountains or the beach?

....

....

....

....

....

❤ Do you like to vacation to a colder climate or a warmer climate?

....

....

....

....

....

....

❤ Do you prefer to dress up or dress down?

....

....

....

....

....

....

....

Make memories. Create connections. Leave a lasting legacy. **133**

❤ Do you like surprises?

....

....

....

....

....

....

....

❤ Can you keep a secret?

....

....

....

....

....

....

....

❤ Do you like being alone or with a group?

....

....

....

....

....

....

....

❤ Is your glass half empty or half full?

....

....

....

....

....

....

....

❤ Are you shy or outgoing?

....

....

....

....

....

....

....

❤ What kinds of snacks do you like?

....

....

....

....

....

....

....

My husband thinks that health food is anything he eats before the expiration date.

~ Rita Rudner

❤ What is your favorite hot beverage?

....

....

....

....

....

....

❤ What is your favorite cold beverage?

....

....

....

....

....

....

💗 Is your favorite meal breakfast, lunch or dinner?

....

....

....

....

....

....

💗 What do you like on your hamburgers?

....

....

....

....

....

....

❤ What is your favorite fruit?

....

....

....

....

....

....

....

There are more than
100 varieties of
bananas, some even
have red skin.

❤ What is your favorite vegetable?

....

....

....

....

....

....

....

❤ What is your favorite food ... and your least favorite?

....

....

....

....

....

....

❤ Do you like food hot & spicy or mild?

....

....

....

....

....

....

❤ What do you like on your pizza?

....

....

....

....

....

....

....

Americans, on the
average, eat 18 acres
of pizza every day.

❤ What is your favorite ice cream topping?

....

....

....

....

....

....

....

❤ **What is your favorite sport to watch?**

....

....

....

....

....

....

....

Sports serve society by providing vivid examples of excellence.

~ George F. Will

❤ **What is your favorite sport to play?**

....

....

....

....

....

....

....

❤ Do you like to read?

....

....

....

....

....

....

....

If you like to read, what types of books do you prefer?

....

....

....

❤ Are you creative or analytical?

....

....

....

....

....

....

....

❤ Can you swim?

....

....

....

....

....

....

....

❤ Have you ever done a flip off a diving board?

....

....

....

....

....

❤ For what did you ever win a ribbon or a trophy?

....

....

....

....

....

....

❤ Do you talk to yourself out loud?

....

....

....

....

....

....

❤ In your family, are you the oldest, youngest, middle, in-between, or only child?

If you're in-between, where are you in the order?

....

....

....

....

....

....

....

....

....

❤ Are you a doer or a procrastinator?

....

....

....

....

....

....

....

❤ Do you remember other people's names or faces best?

....

....

....

....

....

....

❤ Are you patient or impatient?

....

....

....

....

....

....

❤ Do you enjoy learning?

....

....

....

....

....

....

....

Good, better, best,
never let it rest,
until your good is
better, and
your better, best.

~ Aunt Dorothy

❤ What was your favorite subject in school?

....

....

....

....

....

....

....

❤ Are you a list maker?

....

....

....

....

....

....

....

❤ Are you organized or disorganized?

....

....

....

....

....

....

Make memories. Create connections. Leave a lasting legacy.

❤ Use this space for anything else you may want to share.

....

....

....

....

....

....

....

....

....

....

....

....

....

....

About the author

Vickie Mullins is the compassionate, driving force behind the
I Want You To Know Me ... series.

Her professional writing passions run deep. She started
her writing career with inspiration from a high school
journalism class. Her writing talent and interest carried her
through college and evolved into her founding in 1991 Mullins
Creative, Inc., an award-winning, full-service communications
production company.

In 2005, following the publishing of her first book, Vickie
became a sought-after speaker, traveling nationally to share her
message on family legacies. As a member of National Speakers
Association, Vickie is also known for her enthusiastic
presentations on business communications and special market
sales for authors and publishers.

Living in Scottsdale, Ariz. Vickie and husband, Jack, are parents
to grown children, Jonathan and Shannon. They spend many
hours volunteering for the American Diabetes Association and
numerous programs through their church.

If you like this book, you'll love Vickie's presentations.

You may contact her by:

Voice: 480-941-8202

4848 E. Cactus., Suite 505-118
Scottsdale, AZ 85254-4163

email: Vickie@IWantYouToKnowMe.com

www.IWantYouToKnowMe.com